Picture Books
Illustrated by Joe Lasker

•

Big Lion, Little Lion by Miriam Schlein
How Do I Feel? by Norma Simon
My House by Miriam Schlein
Night Lights by Joel Rothman
The Way Mothers Are by Miriam Schlein
What Do I Do? by Norma Simon
What Do I Say? by Norma Simon
When Grandpa Wore Knickers by
   Fern Brown and Andrée Vilas Grabe

MOTHERS CAN DO ANYTHING
Words and Pictures by Joe Lasker

Albert Whitman & Company, Chicago

TO MILLIE

Library of Congress Cataloging in Publication Data

Lasker, Joe.
   Mothers can do anything.

   SUMMARY: Text and illustrations demonstrate many
occupations of mothers including plumber, dentist,
subway conductor, and others.
   1. Woman—Employment—United States—Juvenile
literature. 2. Mothers—Juvenile literature.
(1. Mothers. 2. Occupations) I. Title.
HD6055.L33   331.4'3'0973   72-83684
ISBN 0-8075-5287-9

Fifth Printing 1981

Text and Illustrations ©1972 by Joe Lasker
Published simultaneously in Canada by George J. McLeod, Limited, Toronto
Lithographed in the U.S.A.   All Rights Reserved

Mothers
can do
lots of things.

My mother is a policewoman.

She used to drive a taxi.

My principal is a mother.

My aunt stays home and paints.

The mother next door skates.

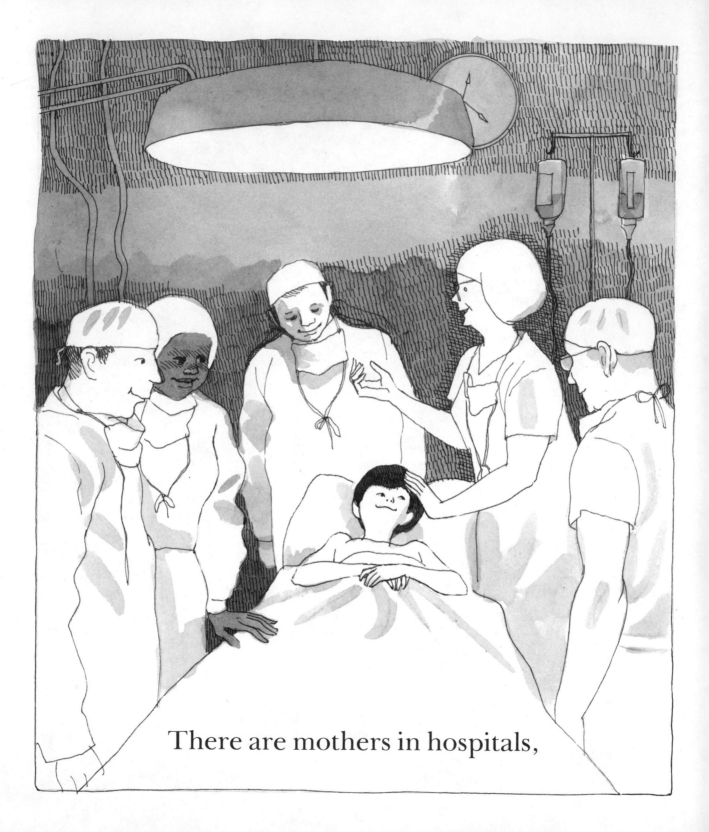

There are mothers in hospitals,

and in courtrooms.

Mothers on courts,

and in ditches.

Grandmothers build big houses.
(No more waiting for Little Red Riding Hood!)

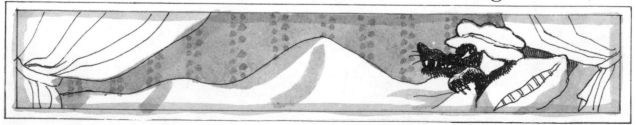

Mothers make films.

Or work in a zoo—

where there's plenty to do.

Mothers fix pipes.

Mothers fix teeth.

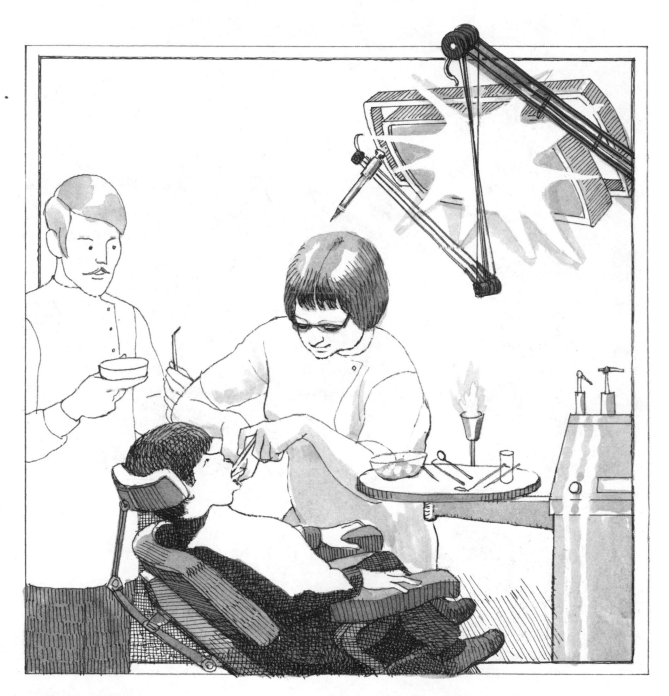

Mothers conduct in halls,

and in trains.

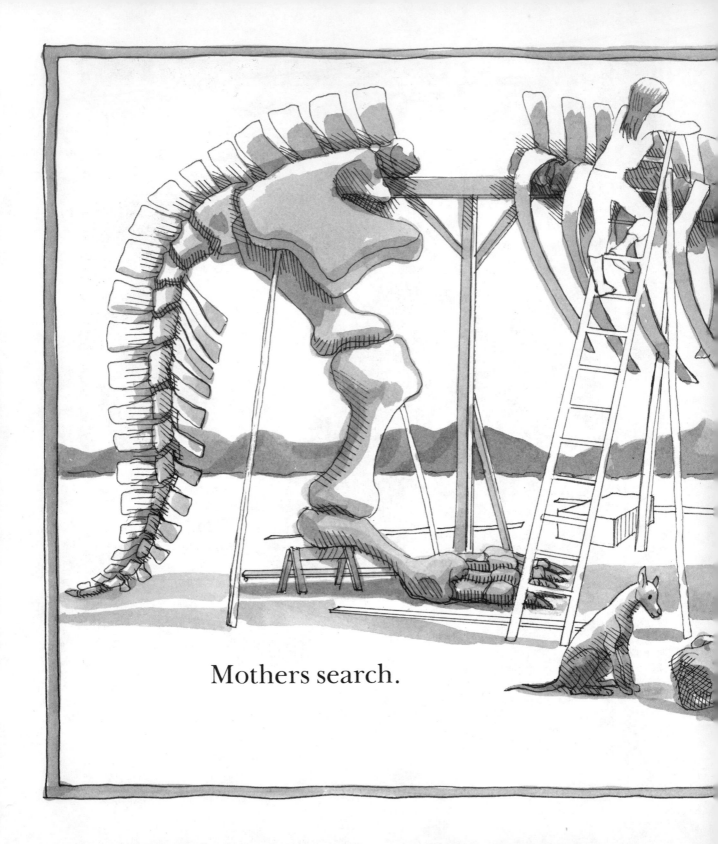

Mothers search.

Do research,

and cook up a stew.

They can hook up a line.

And deliver on time.

Tiger, tiger, cool and bright!

Open wide. Do not bite.

This mother floats with ease.

This one follows a beat.

She dives.

She flies.

She leaps.

She climbs.

Mothers can do anything!

Joe Lasker's illustrations have brought warmth, strength, and humorous observation to many picture books for young children. But until *Mothers Can Do Anything,* Joe Lasker felt his role in books was to present ideas visually, not in words.

The concept of a book of his own grew as Joe Lasker painted in the studio of his Norwalk, Connecticut, home. He found himself listening day after day to women in a radio discussion of problems stemming from the old stereotypes of woman's role and limitations. He realized that here was subject matter for a picture book—a book that would show vocations and avocations mothers follow. He painted mothers in glamorous ballet dresses and in conductor's caps on subways. He sketched young women and older women, pretty ones and plain ones. He chose women whom children regularly see, teachers, policewomen, dentists, and some rarely seen, research workers, painters, tennis players. And he kept emphasis on the closest relationship, mothering.

For Joe Lasker, the question of what to be was never in doubt. Art was to be his career. When he was a boy, his free time was filled with drawing, walking, and reading. He won his first art prize, a medal, when he was a third-grader in a Brooklyn school. Among his favorite books were those illustrated by N. C. Wyeth.

At Cooper Union Art School in New York City there was much to learn. As his work gained depth and quality, Joe Lasker won a Prix de Rome Fellowship and a Guggenheim. He studied and painted in Europe and Mexico. Today his paintings are owned by museums and he regularly has one-man shows in New York and Philadelphia. He is a member of the National Academy of Design.

Mr. and Mrs. Lasker have two sons and a daughter. Mrs. Lasker teaches children with learning problems, and it is to her that this book is dedicated.